MAPLE SYRUP
from the
SUGARHOUSE

Laurie Lazzaro Knowlton   pictures by **Kathryn Mitter**

Albert Whitman & Company
Chicago, Illinois

Thanks, God, and for the loves of my life, Tom,
Charlotte, Jason, Gwen, Kelsey, and Farra—LLK

Library of Congress Cataloging-in-Publication data is on file with the publisher.

Text copyright © 2017 by Laurie Lazzaro Knowlton
Pictures copyright © 2017 by Kathryn Mitter
Published in 2017 by Albert Whitman & Company
ISBN 978-0-8075-7943-5

Printed in China
10 9 8 7 6 5 4 3 2 1 HH 22 21 20 19 18 17

Design by Ellen Kokontis

For more information about Albert Whitman & Company,
visit our website at www.albertwhitman.com.

Maple trees slumber while the winter winds whistle and whirl. Until...

Kelsey feels the sun pushing the cold aside and sees the
snow melting,
     drip,
       drop,
         dripping.
           And the ground below thaws.

"Is the weather right for a sap run?" Kelsey asks.

Daddy nods. "Freezing nights and warmer days..."

Kelsey follows Daddy, trudging out to the woods filled with sugar maple trees.

Daddy says, "Since last year's harvest, the maple trees have grown and stored summer's sugar through the chilly fall and icy winter. That stored sugar is now ready to be collected."

Daddy stops at a maple tree.
"Where is last year's hole?" Kelsey asks.
"It's healed over like the scrape on your knee."
Daddy drills a pencil-sized hole into the giant sugar maple tree.

Kelsey hammers a metal spile into the hole with a tap, tap, tap. Then she hangs the first metal bucket.

Sap droplets drip,
        ting,
           ting-a-ling,
              a-ling!
"We need to keep moving," Daddy says. "We've got the whole sugar bush to tap."

All day, the trees drink up moisture through their roots from the freshly thawed dirt.

All day, the sugar-rich drops of sap drip,

drop,

drop,

drip out of the spiles and into the buckets.

All day and into the next day, the sugar bush camp grows. Momma welcomes grandparents, aunties, uncles, cousins, and friends, who bring food-filled coolers and helping hands.

While Kelsey waits for the sap to fill the buckets, she helps sterilize bottles and stack wood by the firebox, and then plays tag with her cousins, Farra and Gwen. Until...

"Daddy, the buckets are full!" Kelsey announces.

Throughout the sugar bush, everyone works together. Some gather the filled buckets, while others lift the buckets and pour the sap into the storage tank on the back of the tractor.

Kelsey leads Farra and Gwen to return the empty buckets back to the
maple trees' spiles. Then everyone moves to the next section of trees. Until…

Hours later the buckets have been emptied and the holding tank is full. Kelsey hears the tank's sap splish-splash-sloshing all the way to the sugarhouse.

There, Daddy starts the pump to suction the sap through a filter into a larger holding tank. Gravity pulls the sap down through a pipe to a long, flat warming pan.

Below the pan, flames from the firebox heat the chilly, colorless sap, sending it swirling into the evaporator.

"How long before it boils?" Kelsey asks.

"Soon," Daddy says.

Kelsey watches the maple steam roll, rising to the roof vent, then out to the night sky. "Look Daddy, the sap's rumbling, bubbling, boiling!"

"The water in the sap is evaporating, raising the sugar content." Daddy smiles.

Kelsey passes wood to Daddy to refill the stove, keeping the fire white-hot. Momma passes out hot cocoa, and everyone tells stories to pass the time.

More sap is added,
gallon,
after gallon,
after gallon.

Little by little, the sap changes from clear to golden amber.

Daddy takes a spoon and places a drop of sap from the steaming evaporator pan onto his sugar gauge. He checks to see if enough water has evaporated to leave maple syrup.

Everyone waits.
But Daddy shakes his head. "We need to keep boiling."

An hour later Daddy tests the sap again. "We're getting closer."

The rumbling of the boiling sap is the only sound now. Everyone snuggles in sleeping bags, and the adults take turns helping Daddy keep the fire hot.

Until...

Daddy tries again. "It's maple syrup! Time to pour!"
Daddy opens the pour valve on the end of the evaporator.
The sap flows down through a filter into the canning pan.

Everyone jumps into action.
Filling bottles.

Twisting caps.

Line them up.

Yay!

Until the first run of maple syrup is bottled and cooling.

Kelsey and Daddy sit down with family and friends to enjoy a breakfast feast of pancakes,

sausage, biscuits,

coffee, and ice cream!

All smothered in liquid-gold maple syrup.

Kelsey snuggles up with a blanket while the morning birds chirp. She dreams about the sleeping maple trees awakening, singing their ting-a-ling drip, drop song until…

the buckets fill again.

Marvelous Maple Syrup Facts

- The history of making maple syrup is older than our country. Native Americans gathered maple tree sap in wooden buckets and used heated rocks to boil down the sap to make maple syrup.

- Maple syrup is made in Canada and the United States. The following states produce maple syrup: Connecticut, Illinois, Indiana, Iowa, Kentucky, Maine, Maryland, Massachusetts, Michigan, Minnesota, Missouri, New Hampshire, New Jersey, New York, North Carolina, Ohio, Pennsylvania, Rhode Island, Tennessee, Vermont, Virginia, West Virginia, and Wisconsin. The Canadian provinces that produce maple syrup are: New Brunswick, Nova Scotia, Ontario, Prince Edward Island, and Quebec.

- Maple syrup season usually happens between February and March. The weather dictates when maple syrup harvest will happen. The days when the temperature is above freezing signal the trees to drink moisture from the thawing ground. Sugar stored from the past summer moves up through the tree with the moisture. The season ends when the weather pattern changes and the buds on the maple tree pop.

- A sugar bush can range in size. One can be as small as fifty trees or as large as thousands of trees.

- The maple syrup process begins by locating trees that are at least 12" in diameter. Each tree is then "tapped" by drilling a hole 1.5–2" deep. Then a metal straw-like spile is tapped into the tree with a hammer. The spiles do not permanently hurt the trees. At the end of the season, the spiles are pulled out and the trees regrow, much like our skin repairs itself from a cut.

- Each tree will give up approximately 10–18 gallons of sap per season. When the sap comes out of the tree, only 1–3% is sugar. The rest is water. The sap needs to boil to evaporate the water and leave a sugar content of 67%. It takes about 40–50 gallons of sap to make one gallon of syrup. That is about a full bathtub of sap to make one gallon of maple syrup.

- Unopened maple syrup has a long shelf life of up to a year if kept in a cool, dark area. If placed in a freezer, the syrup will last indefinitely. After a container is opened, it must be refrigerated, and the syrup will usually stay fresh for six months to a year.

- If you are interested in participating in the maple syrup experience, check with county extension services located in maple syrup states to see when they have their maple syrup season demonstrations. Many towns also have maple syrup fairs.